365 WAYS TO LOVE YOUR WIFE

A Respect Dare Resource

365 WAYS TO LOVE YOUR WIFE

© 2014 Nina Roesner. All rights reserved. No portion of this book may be reproduced, stored in a retrieval system, or transmitted in any form or by any means – electronic, mechanical, photocopy, recording, or any other – except for brief quotations in printed reviews, without the prior permission of the publisher.

Published by Greater Impact, 554 Belle Meade Farm Drive, Loveland, OH, 45140.

Scriptures are taken from the following: The Holy Bible, New International Version. Copyright © 1973, 1978, 1984, International Bible Society. Used by permission of Zondervan Bible Publishers. The Holy Bible, New Living Translation®. Copyright © 1996. Used by permission of Tyndale House Publishers, Inc., Wheaton, Illinois 60189. All rights reserved. The New American Standard Bible®. Copyright © 1960, 1962, 1963, 1968, 1971, 1972,1973,1975, 1995 by The Lockman Foundation. Used by permission. The King James Version of the Bible. Public domain. The New King James Version®. Copyright © 1982 by Thomas Nelson, Inc. Used by permission. All rights reserved. The Message by Eugene H. Peterson. Copyright © 1993, 1994, 1995, 1996, 2000, 2001, 2002. Used by permission of NavPress Publishing Group. All rights reserved.

Printed in the United States of America.

365 WAYS TO LOVE YOUR WIFE

A Respect Dare Resource

by Nina Roesner

For God's Men...

Who choose to learn to love, even when it is hard, even when it hasn't been modeled well for you, even when it is risky.

May God bless you for your perseverance and your pursuit of being Christ-like in the way you love.

May you bring glory to our Savior.

Your sons and daughters learn how to give and receive love by watching you – may they see Him in you.

Keep growing.

Respectfully,
Nina

Why Does this Little Book Exist?

Most of the husbands of the wives who do *The Respect Dare* or take Daughters of Sarah® tell us the same thing: *"I am inspired to be a better man because of what she has learned to do for me."*

And on occasion, a husband has also been known to ask, *"How can I better express love to my wife?"* In an effort to help these men, we have put together this small book and list, derived from wives whose husbands have begun demonstrating love more effectively, and from some of the wives on our *Respect Dare* community page on Facebook®.

It is designed not to be 101 different things you can do but provides 365 – one for each day. Please also know ahead of time that some of the items repeat. Many wives would agree with me that hearing, "I love you," once a year is not going to be enough, so we repeat a few of these actions of love so you don't have to remember to do all of them.

You probably don't need me to tell you that God did something interesting when He created women. But what you might not know is that brain research shows that women, generally speaking, have a deeply wired need for *reassurance.* This shows up in a myriad of ways, but here are a few that appear impact YOU because they show up in marriage:

- Reassurance of her importance to you
- Reassurance of physical safety
- Reassurance of financial security
- Reassurance of her attractiveness to you
- Reassurance of your affection for your children

And research tells us that at the core of these is the deep need for reassurance of your love for her. The interesting part is that this reassurance shows up as a frequent need – not once a year on an anniversary, but daily. Research also shows that most of us women have our perceptions of our relationships clouded by our most recent interactions – if there is a lack of positive feelings communicated towards her, she feels (in her heart, mind you, not her head, she's smart enough to know the difference) that she is not loved by you. In other words, we want to know, "Do you think I'm pretty *today*? Do you love me *today*?"

So why is she unhappy? I mean, you are probably working hard to provide a nice life for her and your kids, taking care of things around the house, and doing your best, right?

But she's still unhappy.

So why?

The answer is going to surprise you.

She doesn't *feel* loved by you.

Your wife might know *in her head* that you love her, but if you have a disagreement and you are harsh with her, or if you put her down, or do something discourteous, selfish, or unkind, while she still knows you love her, she is *losing the feeling* that you love her. (I should note that this is different than the "settling" that most marriages go through – that infatuation stage should grow into mature love). Or if you have certain ways that you show your love for her that are NOT the love language she speaks, it will feel very much to her like you might if this were to happen…

Let's say you are feeling amorous. You approach your wife for intimacy, and she brings you a sandwich instead.

This might be a very nice sandwich, maybe a turkey club with bacon, crisp lettuce, and a tomato and just the right amount of mayo. **But it is not what you want at that moment.** One could even argue that it isn't what you need, either.

Now pretend you spend a decade... ten long years ... wanting, needing, aching for sex ... but each time you approach her for sex, all she does is run off to the kitchen and then bring you a sandwich.

So how would you feel?

Disappointed? Unfulfilled? This is how your wife feels when you show her love, but do it *your way* instead of what *speaks to her heart.*

Because she loves God, she won't just walk away from the marriage until she's in so much pain she feels like there's nothing left to do to escape it. Before she gets to the point of leaving she will eventually become so discouraged and apathetic, that she stops trying, especially if she is working on the marriage and you still are not loving her with what makes her *feel* loved by you. She will also stop trying if you reject her affections for you, or if the majority of communication from you to her is critical or negative in nature. She will wonder why she is bothering. She will feel invisible and alone, and will want to escape these feelings.

She is then fertile soil for the enemy's tricks and might start thinking about divorce or an affair, or just start living a life separate from you.

Based on our discussions with women, we know what they are hoping for, and it is attention and affection from their husbands.

A wife's greatest sorrow is feeling invisible and alone.

And Dr. John Gottman's research (the guy that predicts divorce with 91% accuracy after spending less than 5 minutes with a couple) shows that in 81% of self-destructing couples (those that divorce) the MAN determined the outcome. 65% of the time, he did not search for underlying communication from his wife, but instead responded with a knee-jerk reaction of criticism, defensiveness, contempt, or stonewalling.

He made negative assumptions – about her, about himself, about situations, and did not receive influence from her.

These couples divorced.

And since currently over 60% of divorces are filed by the wife, it is wise of you to stop coasting or worse, being negative, and start doing your best to love your wife well.

You may have heard the old joke about the long-married couple, where the wife asks the husband why he doesn't ever say he loves her – he replies, "I told you that the day we got married 40 years ago. I'll let you know if it changes." **Everyone politely laughs, but most women in the room experience a crack in their hearts – because we all know something you don't…** *most of us don't feel loved by our husbands.*

Sitting in a room full of strangers, I posed this question to 12 publishing company professionals at Thomas Nelson as we discussed my book for wives, "The Respect Dare." One of the marketing people asked, "So this is a book aimed at women who are hurting in their marriages?" I responded, "No, this is a book for all women, because all women feel alone in their marriage. Correct me if I'm wrong, ladies."

And the women in the room all looked down except one – the one woman who was not married! She looked at the other women and her eyes grew wide. I have always felt badly about giving her such a negative view of marriage!

What was interesting, however, is that once the marketing people understood that it literally was nearly all married women, that is how they went about marketing the book.

You might think this "alone-ness" is our problem to figure out, and to a certain degree, it is. I speak to women to help them do what they can to impact their marriages by improving their relationship with God, first. Then I teach them the following:

- How to not have expectations of her husband, but to accept him as he is
- How to submit to him in marriage, being agreeable to him as a person, and voicing disagreements in an agreeable way instead of being contentious
- How to help her husband
- How to take care of things at home, so he has the domestic support he needs to do his job
- How to encourage her husband, to build him up as a man
- How to respect her husband unconditionally, instead of tearing him down

- How to ask for what she needs instead of hoping he will read her mind
- How to be her husband's friend, so he is not feeling alone in life
- How to speak more concisely and intentionally, and less
- How to be content and not complain

But I will tell you honestly, that even if she does all these things, it doesn't let you off the hook. The Bible is very specific – you are to love your wife. You are also called to respect and honor her. You also CAN make an impact in your marriage. And you should. As God would have it, He is not silent on the matter, and He holds you accountable for your family.

There is some specific communication to the Ephesian church in the Bible that pertains to marriage and Christ's relationship with the church. I'm going to give you the verses and then summarize the teaching here. Stick with me. We're getting closer. It will be worth it.

We'll begin with the most important question of your day:

What if God gave you your wife so you could learn how to love Jesus?

1 Peter 3:7 (ESV) *Likewise, husbands, live with your wives in an understanding way, showing honor to the woman as the weaker vessel, since they are heirs with you of the grace of life, so that your prayers may not be hindered.*

When you are harsh with your wife, you are not being loving. **Remember when you first started dating?** Maybe even in the early months or first year of your marriage, how gentle, kind, understanding, and honoring (respectful) you were towards her?

Do you hear that you are damaging your relationship with God when you stop being like this with your wife?

Do you hear that God does not even want to talk to you if you are dishonoring or not understanding towards her? She is as precious to God as you are – and she is your equal in His eyes.

Ephesians 5:22-24 (ESV)

22Wives, submit to your husbands as to the Lord. 23For the husband is the head of the wife as Christ is the head of the church, his body, of which he is the Savior. 24Now as the church submits to Christ, so also wives should submit to their husbands in everything.

The concept of "submission" is a willingness to place ourselves under our husband's leadership in a given situation. It is a CHOICE we make – it's not something you get to force upon your wife, or hold over her head. You don't get to demand submission. **You can lead, but harsh treatment and unloving behavior makes it hard for your wife (or anyone else, for that matter) to follow**. If you find yourself in a mindset of ever thinking, "Why won't that woman submit?!!" you have the wrong attitude. If you are shoving your authority down others' throats, it is not honoring to God. **Jesus, our role model, never did things this way.**

This authority, by the way, is just responsibility – God holds you accountable for your family. He doesn't mean for you to control every little thing in your house. Your wife will probably know more about relationships and your children than you do. If you can't defer to her expertise, or if you view her as "less-than" you, you clearly miss something fundamental. God created man and woman as equal heirs in the sight of Himself. Check 1 Peter 3:7. You are to respect and honor her. And check Genesis 3. **She was created because you need her help.** You are doing your family harm if you are not considering her counsel in decision making. Yes, when you can't agree, you have the final say – but if you are making decisions without including her in them, you are missing a viewpoint that God wants you to have. You should also know that most men and women's brains are wired differently – she is going to have insights you do not.

What the verse in Ephesians 5:23 refers to with regards to the husband being head of the wife, in addition to the responsibility for the family that God has given to you, is that you are the one that "brings life" to your wife – like Christ came to give His church life as a servant-leader. Are you doing that? Do your words and actions bring her life? Or do they bring her discouragement and emotional death? And before you misunderstand something, know that you are responsible to God for your family – she is your equal, but the Genesis 3 account is clear. God holds Adam accountable. And God created Eve out of Adam's rib, instead of out of the dirt, as he created Adam and the animals. But these verses say something completely different than what you may have thought in the past – they are not about ruling over her.

Ephesians 5:25-33 (ESV)

25Husbands, love your wives, just as Christ loved the church and gave himself up for her 26to make her holy, cleansing her by the washing with water through the word, 27and to present her to himself as a radiant church, without stain or wrinkle or any other blemish, but holy and blameless. 28In this same way, husbands ought to love their wives as their own bodies. He who loves his wife loves himself. 29After all, no one ever hated his own body, but he feeds and cares for it, just as Christ does the church— 30for we are members of his body. 31"For this reason a man will leave his father and mother and be united to his wife, and the two will become one flesh." 32This is a profound mystery—but I am talking about Christ and the church. 33However, each one of you also must love his wife as he loves himself, and the wife must respect her husband.

Your love is to be sacrificial toward your wife. That might mean doing things you aren't really comfortable with. Do them anyway. You'll get used to them. Your actions and words are to bring life and take care of your wife. **You are not to be subject to your parents, either – they no longer matter as much as your wife does (leave and cleave).** Yes, your wife is to submit to you when the two of you cannot agree on a decision. And yes, she is to respect you. But even if she's not, you are to behave lovingly toward her.

You are to love her unconditionally, as Christ loves His church, sacrificing Himself for us, loving us regardless of our behavior towards Him. You are not off the hook even if she is not being respectful or submissive.

James 4:17 (NIV) *Anyone, then, who knows the good he ought to do and doesn't do it, sins.*

Are you intentionally withholding love from your wife? Do you know what her love language is? Do you knowingly choose to NOT do things she would consider loving, making excuses for failing to do so? Know this is disobedience, and disobedience is sin.

There is another verse you cannot ignore and need to understand. It has everything to do with mature believers being brother and sister in Christ, representing Him to one another – and how they are to interact with reference to "authority."

I saw this verse played out in an interesting but powerful way many years ago when I was working two jobs. During the day, I did human resources management for a medium sized manufacturing company. At night, I was a trainer for an international communication and public speaking corporation. **I was teaching a public speaking course in my community and my immediate supervisor and his boss, the CEO of the manufacturing company, both signed up for the class.** As the trainer, one of my responsibilities was to coach the participants and help them achieve greater skill level each session. In doing so, I had to put them on the spot in front of about 40 people, literally stopping them mid-sentence, and having them try something new to help them be more skilled as speakers. With my superiors in the class, I wondered how this would impact our work relationships – and it was amazing to me that it literally had no impact at all. Both of these men did everything I asked them to do, and we all grew as a result. **In the classroom, they actively put themselves in a position of submission to my authority, although none of us ever talked about it, and their attitude made all the difference in the world.**

This was an interesting experience for me, as several years before, I had a Christian male in a class and he actively refused my attempts to coach him. **This created a difficult dynamic in my classroom with this one class member actively refusing to try something new, simply because I was female.** His employer was displeased with his performance at work (the lack of improvement) and I had several conversations with him and his boss about the situation. I could offer up suggestions or try to help him improve, but if he refused to accept or receive my coaching, that was entirely up to him. He eventually complained to my boss about the class and how the course violated his religious beliefs because he was "under the authority of a woman." My boss graciously gave the company their money back and asked him not to return to class. I later learned he was fired. Ironically, the supervisor who terminated him was a man. **I was told that this man's inability to learn from others was a major issue for him at work – most of his relationships were filled with disdain and contempt for those he perceived as "less than" himself.** Obviously not very Christ-like behavior, regardless of one's views about male superiority – Christ was clearly superior to the disciples, but He washed their feet.

We are to behave likewise.

Ephesians 5:21 says, "submit to one another out of reverence for Christ."

I admired my boss and our CEO for the humble way they asked for help and I respectfully gave it to them. I tried to help the Christian man in my class, but he refused – because I was a woman. He took 1 Timothy 2:12 literally, which reads "But I do not allow a woman to teach or exercise authority over a man, but to remain quiet."

I will also admit to you that I struggled with my attitude toward him. His behavior and attitude were a disruption to the class.

The extent to which a husband has this same attitude is the extent to which his wife will feel invisible, alone, and hurting in their marriage – or the extent to which she feels valued, cherished, and loved.

I have seen husbands who take this verse so literally that they will not be alone with their children when they are young, because they may need to hear instructions for how to care for a nursing baby from a woman, their wife. I would like to think that most of us would agree that is simply ridiculous, but alas, there are still those out there today who view women as second class citizens. If we remember Christ's washing of the disciple's feet, we can see these men's attitude says more about their pride than the women they claim to be superior to, though, doesn't it?

I am not here to discuss women teaching in church. I am aware that many male pastors feel it sinful to even read theology written by women. There are those who feel women should not work and lead others in business, although God gives us the entrepreneurial example of the Proverbs 31 woman, and Deborah as a judge. Several women also had house churches in New Testament times, and there's enough argument on both sides of the fence within the conservative community to make one seriously wonder what the Truth is. Know, however, that a woman's role in the church is often extrapolated to mean similar things in the family, which I would suggest should not be the case.

We must also not forget the story of Sapphira and Ananais. They conspired to lie to Peter about how much money they received from selling land and giving it to the church. **Ananais was rebuked by Peter and struck dead by God.** Three hours later, Sapphira does what she and her husband agreed upon with Peter – in other words, she submitted to her husband and lied – and God also used Peter to rebuke her and then struck her dead as well. It should also be noted that this is the same Peter who gives instructions to wives in 1 Peter 3:1-6 to submit to their husbands!

Those who endorse the full silence of women and suggest they are not put in positions of authority or leadership often fail to explain or even talk about Sapphira's submission in Acts 5. I believe there is no better example in the Bible of how a woman is to submit to God first, and to her husband with a gentle attitude second, but in obedience to God alone.

Most in the western world have decided to follow the Bible in this way: the Old Testament describes the character of God, the New Testament gives salvation and the example of Jesus (God) for us to model our lives after, specifically in the gospels, following His words, and the other books are contextual documents that speak into our lives in different ways. **Regardless of where one lands in the debate on gender and teaching, the fact remains that a woman knows best what makes her feel loved – it is a mystery men want to understand, and most often, cannot explain to each other.** I am humbled to provide a bit of assistance to you in this area. I admire you even more as a man for seeking to be a better husband and father.

Now check what Jesus Himself says to the Ephesian Church in Revelation 2:

2I know your deeds, your hard work and your perseverance. I know that you cannot tolerate wicked men, that you have tested those who claim to be apostles but are not, and have found them false. 3You have persevered and have endured hardships for my name, and have not grown weary.

4Yet I hold this against you: You have forsaken your first love. 5Remember the height from which you have fallen! Repent and do the things you did at first. If you do not repent, I will come to you and remove your lampstand from its place.

Jesus is telling you (and your wife) that He understands how hard you have worked. He knows you have been at it for a long time. He knows you haven't given up yet. He knows that you have suffered for His name. He knows this. But in His heart, **He wants you to know that He has something against you: You have forsaken your first love**. He wants you to do the things you did at first in your relationship with Him. He wants you to remember, daily, the depravity of your soul, the depth of your sin, and respond with repentance, worship and love for Him at the great gift He gives to you. He wants to be first in your life, not in the immature infatuation sense, but rather in the deep, steadfast, mature, focused love of Him as the most important One in your life sense. **If you do not, He will issue a consequence. Understand this: Repentance is not repentance without changed behavior.**

Do not miss that this is the Ephesian Church. Most Bible teachers use these verses in application to marriage, also. And there is research that demonstrates that to reignite your marriage relationship, one of the most helpful things you can do *is do what you did in the beginning.*

Your wife's heart is similar to God's.

She needs daily reassurance of your love. Your God wants daily pursuance of Him. Your wife understands this – that's why it's easier for her to connect with God and develop her relationship. You can read more about the differences in how God created men and women by reading *"Why Respect Him?"* on my blog at www.NinaRoesner.com.

If you literally don't know what to do to begin to show your wife your love, I'd like to highly recommend *The Love Dare* book by the Kendrick brothers. It's awesome. They even have an app for your phone. I'd also recommend reading the list I'm giving you as a daily thing to do. You can also sign up for our texting application on my website at www.NinaRoesner.com – you'll get a text a day of one of these things you can DO to show your wife your love. I'd also highly recommend asking your wife. For me, and many women, it's really just a couple of little things – **but each day**, so don't think this is uber hard and scary.

Double dog dare you to beg God to help you love your wife so she feels loved by you.

It will change everything.

His love always does.

One last thing before I give you the list... know that YOU and your opinions matter deeply to your wife. And the opinion that matters most to her is what **you** think of **her.**

She is wired differently than you – she needs (often deeply needs) **daily** affirmation and re-affirmation of her place in your heart.

Many women also appreciate affection in front of others – because women know that their kids are learning how God loves His children, and they want you to model affection in marriage for your kids. They also like others to know that they are loved – it is a self-esteem boost for them. We know most men are fine with the "I love you" spoken to you on your wedding day, but women simply aren't wired like that. We wonder daily whether you think we are still attractive to you, talented, smart, competent, and whether you are still in love with us. Thirty years into our marriages, we STILL want to feel special to you. An anniversary card once a year just doesn't communicate that.

Some men understand this best when I liken affection to sexual intimacy – if we had sex once and expected that to be enough for you for 30 years, you might not be able to thrive in that environment. The same applies to your wife and how she needs to feel loved by you **daily.**

Often, she'll be more motivated to give you what you need when you give her what she needs. ☺

In this day and age, more and more of the women we work with are having online affairs that often evolve into physical encounters. **A smart husband will put some effort into keeping his wife feeling precious to him – think of it like building a fence around the sanctity of your marriage.** Yes, it IS our sin if we stray, but you can do something to make it easier for us to keep our hearts at home. Just like your wife is not responsible for any pornography use of her husband, she can make it easier for him to not sin in that regard by staying fit and meeting her husband's physical needs. Most of us ladies do not understand that thing about guys, either, but those of us who are wise are happy to keep you happy, whether we understand it or not. Won't you do the same for us, but in a different area?

Know too, that according to 1 Peter 3:7 **the effectiveness of your prayers is actually at stake**: *Husbands, in the same way, treat your wives with consideration as the weaker partners and show them honor as fellow heirs of the grace of life. In this way nothing will hinder your prayers.*

Your wife has probably already told you what speaks deeply to her heart. If you will but demonstrate love to her, removing her fears of position in your heart or security, you will both represent Christ and His church to the world.

So, with great admiration and sincere hope and prayer that these impact your marriage as you daily apply them, learn and grow, I respectfully present you with THE LIST…

365 Ways to Love Your Wife:

1. Take your forefinger and brush her hair out of her eyes behind her ear when listening to her. Or just run your fingers through her hair if it is short. A gentle touch like this goes a long way.

2. Pay her a compliment daily about her character – women are wired to evaluate the state of their relationships on a daily, versus long-term, basis. Keep her confident in your care for her by paying her a compliment once a day. Say something like, "I was just admiring how you (insert something good here, like: keep going after a long day, show such tenderness to our kids, are so tidy in the kitchen, are so good with animals, are so giving of your time, are so organized, balance so many things, stay in such good shape, etc.) with so much on your plate. I think you are amazing!" Or end with, "I love how well you love us."

3. Do a daily devotional somewhat consistently. She deeply wants you to grow as a Christian man (this impacts her level of trust in your decisions).

4. Let her know what God is teaching you once in a while.

5. Switch your daily devotional out for *The Love Dare* twice a year, or better yet, sign up for our texting app on my website at www.NinaRoesner.com, or do one dare a week from *The Love Dare* book throughout the year. Repeat, changing things up just a bit to keep it interesting.

6. Send a text message during the day – something like any of the following:

- Just thinking about U.
- Can't wait 2 C U tonight.
- Just daydreaming about U.
- How is it that you are so smart?
- Thinking about UR lovely face & U made me ☺ (leave out the other body parts – it makes us feel more valuable to not talk about those! Most women also like to be told we are beautiful – and we deeply want to know that we are attractive to YOU)
- It was smart of you to (insert last money saving thing she did). Thank you!
- Looking forward to another one of your amazing dinners!
- YOU. Can't stop thinking about you.
- Thinking about you... totally distracting me. ☺
- Miss you. Like right now. ☺
- Why are you so pretty?
- I was remembering how we went (somewhere together that she enjoyed). That still makes me ☺!
- Can't wait to give you a big kiss when I get home.
- XOXO !!
- Doing okay?
- Praying for your day right now.

7. Leave her a voice mail when you know she is tied up or does not have her phone, something romantic like, "I just wanted to hear your voice."

8. Gently rub the back of her neck or shoulders when seated next to her, if she likes to be touched.
9. Pick up after yourself.
10. Clean out her car for her.
11. After one of the kids' performances or report cards, tell or text her, "I love how you pour yourself into our kids! Little Joey's play last night was an example of that. He did better because you cheered him on."
12. If she is working out or trying to eat right and exercise, make sure you tell her how proud of her you are and how hard you know it is.
13. Change the oil in her car, or do regular maintenance – it makes her feel taken care of by you.
14. Lock up the house at night so she does not have to do it.
15. Tuck your kids into bed, even if she does it, too. Research shows women view fathers who are involved with their children, favorably.
16. If smoke or smells or noises bother her, protect her from them – blow out the candle in another room, don't wear heavy cologne, don't use heavy air fresheners in your car. Research shows women have more sensitive senses of smell, sight, and hearing than men.
17. Make time on a regular basis to be with just her.
18. Hold her hand in public.
19. Kiss her in public, if she is okay with that. If she's not, just put your arm around her waist. Chances are she will love others knowing she is loved.
20. Pick up toys with the kids without being asked. She will appreciate "help" and not think you think she

can't handle things herself. She does not think like you do.

21. Kiss the nape of her neck and kiss her there while she is standing.
22. Ask her to teach you how to do your little girl's hair.
23. Show her the photos you keep on your computer of your family. If you don't have any, add some, then show her. Use one as a screen saver if you can.
24. Call her name from across the room, then tell her, "I just wanted to see your lovely face."
25. Bring her a little gift once a month or so – even a single flower, her favorite candy bar, book, coffee, etc. and present it to her in a sweet way (maybe holding the flower out to her and saying, "This is nowhere near as pretty as you are, but it made me think of you anyway.").
26. Leave her a little note in her underwear drawer. Be classy with whatever you write.
27. Hug her for no reason and with no motive every day. If you only touch her when you want sex, she will feel used and insignificant to you. When she feels like your treasure, your precious gem, she will be delighted more often, and work harder on her end of the relationship and her responsibilities. She will also trust you more, which means she will be less inhibited in the bedroom.
28. Avoid pornography and teach your sons to do the same. If you are caught up in this, get free, or get help if you can't. She would feel betrayed if she knew you looked at other women in any way.

29. Be proactive about taking care of work around the house, the budget, and spending time with the family – every week. Make it a habit.
30. Take her shopping and buy her a new outfit once in a while – or give her a gift card for a store and one for a nearby coffee shop for her and a friend, then watch the kids while she goes.
31. Make sure she feels encouraged to update her wardrobe – frugal women can get by on $100 a year for clothes if they have a good quality base.
32. Take her on a moon light walk. Compliment her and listen well. Hold her hand. Stop once in a while just to kiss her.
33. If she ever gets mad enough to walk out, go after her. Tell her, "I can't live without you. I'm sorry things escalated so much – come back. Let's talk through this."
34. Hold her hand while you walk next to each other.
35. Make dinner once a week (or more if you love doing that).
36. Bring her a cup of tea or coffee in the morning sometimes.
37. Ask her if she'll do a devotion with you – even if it is an online one and you do it separately and you just ask her, "What did you get from today's devotion?"
38. Meet her after work somewhere for an inexpensive dinner once a week.
39. Stroke or brush her hair.
40. Take her hand at church during worship or prayer.
41. Open doors for her.
42. Notice when she has her arms full and say, "Here, let me get this for you!"

43. Never go through a door first, or leave her behind you when you go somewhere.
44. Help her with her coat.
45. Don't conduct male body grooming sessions where she can see, smell, or hear you.
46. Switch off the phone or ignore it when you are together.
47. Make eye contact with her when she is speaking to you.
48. Replay back to her what you think she said – especially if she tells you she is hurting about something – especially if she thinks it is your fault.
49. Say I'm sorry when you hurt her without explaining why you did it or why it is her fault.
50. Hold her when she cries.
51. Take a Sunday school class with her.
52. Let her know verbally that she is any one of these things to you: precious, a treasure, special, important, a gift, the best...
53. Hold her hand in the middle of the night.
54. Ask her how her day went and really listen, asking questions.
55. Wink at her across a room or via text. ☺
56. Deal with the kids one day a weekend, or get them ready for school.
57. Be quiet when getting ready so she can get needed sleep (women actually need more than men).
58. Let her get a nap.
59. Give her a kiss after holding her car door open for her.
60. Leave her a note if you leave before she does that just tells her she's special to you.

61. Smile at her. A lot.
62. Smile at your kids. A lot.
63. Gently but firmly stand up for her with your kids.
64. Don't criticize her in front of the kids – it undermines her authority.
65. There are some things that you will need to stand firm on – be sure you have prayed about these things and let her know this and that you feel led to make the decision. If you feel led by God, do not give in to her.
66. Ask her to pray for you about what you are going through.
67. Ask her what she thinks – and really consider it, especially when it comes to relationships and kids. She sees, hears, and picks up on subtle cues more than you do – if you are both average male and female, so says the research.
68. Rub her feet. Tell her you think she has beautiful toes. Feel free to nibble on them, unless she does not like it.
69. Make a list of 30 little things you did while dating and put them on your calendar each year to do again.
70. Pick her up off her feet and swing her around once in a while.
71. Dance with her when there is no music. When she says she doesn't hear music, tell her you always hear music when you are together.
72. Take care of yourself physically by staying in (or getting in) shape and seeing the doctor. She worries about your health.

73. Get control of your anger, if you struggle with it. When she is afraid of you, it destroys your relationship.
74. Ask her if you drink, if you drink too much. Then listen. Take action if she says, "yes."
75. Bring her chicken soup if she's sick. Better yet, take the day off if you can to let her sleep and you take care of her and the kids.
76. Ask her to find you a highly rated book on being a better dad or husband – then read it and implement what you read.
77. When she seems angry (does not mean she is, btw) and says something sarcastic or hurtful or disrespectful to you, gently take her hands in yours and say, "Honey, I know you didn't mean that. I can see you are hurting. Let's talk about this. I want to understand."
78. Offer to take the baby when he is fussy or sick so she can rest. Make sure you do not allow him to cry, or put him in front of the TV, but rather interact with him.
79. Help her know how to teach you how to do baby care by saying, "I'm not real good at this, but I want to learn. Can you watch me do it and just coach me so I can practice?"
80. Tell or text to her that she is a good mom – and be specific about something she did that brings that to light.
81. Tell or text to her that she is a good wife and that you'd be lost without her.
82. Ask her if there's anything you can do for her this weekend.

83. Learn her love language (or ask her if you cannot figure it out) and do a little research on how to show love to someone who is that language. Make a list of 50 neat things you could do for her – ask her for help if you need to.
84. Pray for and with her. This can be one of the most intimate things you do together. Your marriage and your kids need this kind of attention.
85. Nibble on her earlobe when you greet her while giving her a hug.
86. Nuzzle her neck when hugging her.
87. Hug her from behind when she is standing at the sink or changing table.
88. Carry the laundry baskets upstairs for her without being asked.
89. Always thank her for making dinner and find something to compliment about the meal.
90. Run your finger along her jawline, starting at her ear, brush her lips, then down her neck to her collarbone, and stop at her shoulder.
91. Using your finger, lift her head with her chin, and brush her lips gently with yours.
92. Use breath mints frequently – and deodorant. Peppermint oil on the tongue is an inexpensive long lasting solution, also.
93. Offer to drive the kids where they need to go on the weekend.
94. Stare at her until she notices. When she asks you what you are doing, say something like, "I just can't get over how gorgeous you are."

95. Insist that she takes time to read a book, spend time with her girlfriends, or whatever else fills her up.
96. Buy her a little jewelry item for no reason – unless she is not into jewelry.
97. If she has a hobby, even one that does not include you, get her a little gift that supports it.
98. If her shoes are scuffed, polish them for her without saying anything. It might take her a little while to notice, especially if she is a working busy mom.
99. When she complains, empathize. Saying, "Oh, I'm so sorry! That must be hard for you. Is there anything I can do to help?"
100. Take her out to dinner. After you are seated, make extended eye contact with her. Say something like, "You are the most stunning woman in the room tonight."
101. Tell or text her, "I'm so glad you are our kids' mom. You really know them."
102. Dip her backwards next time you kiss her.
103. Go to bed when she does. Don't always watch TV or play video games, but talk to her and maybe even pray with her instead.
104. If she complains about herself, take her by the shoulders and say something like, "Look at me. That's not true. You are lovely. You are worthy. You are highly valued by God and me. No more lies." Then kiss her gently.
105. Continue doing these things until they become habits. Commit to continuing to grow as a husband and don't stop trying to communicate love to your

wife. She needs it daily. Like you need respect. Like you both need air.

106.   Tell her, "I'm so glad I married such a smart woman." Point out things that demonstrate her brainpower.

107.   Be kind in how you talk about her parents and yours.

108.   Agree upon a dollar amount each of you can spend without talking to the other person, then follow it.

109.   If you have small children, don't make your wife carry the car seat with the baby in it.

110.   If your wife criticizes you, evaluate what she says to find the truth in it, instead of getting defensive.

111.   Ask God to conform you into the image of Christ, then obey Him by studying the Bible and acting on what you read.

112.   Text her, "I love how you pour into our family, part of why they did great is because of you," after a kid performance.

113.   Remember - loving your wife well is NOT about changing her, but rather about becoming more loving as a man and dad.

114.   Take a deep look at your wife's face. Is she still happy looking? Or sad? Ask God what He would reveal to you.

115.   Tell your wife and kids something once, maybe twice. You create passive resistance when you hound your kids and your wife about something.

116.   Do the right thing. Even if it is hard. Always. She'll admire you for it.

117. Don't brag about yourself, but let her know, "Hey God did this cool thing," and let her celebrate with you.
118. Ask God to give you peace. Don't let your stress work you and your family into an anxious frenzy.
119. If you often frown or complain about food your wife makes, you will find yourself with boring food. She'll quit trying.
120. If you want a dessert and you are with your family, make sure you get one for everyone and not just yourself.
121. Know she reads your social media. Post about how blessed you are to be married to her at least once a month.
122. Lock up the house at night so she doesn't have to.
123. Time your communication well. Don't bring up something difficult when she's had a rough day.
124. Text her, "YOU are the most gorgeous woman in the room, any day. Miss you. Love you."
125. Ask her to pray for you about something you are dealing with right now. Then let her know how it went.
126. Put "You make a great friend," on her Facebook wall.
127. Tuck your kids into bed at night, every single night, even if she does it too.
128. Pray with the kids at bedtime. Know your wife gets a "warm fuzzy" every time you do.
129. If smoke, smells, noise, etc., bothers her, protect her from them.

130. Be gentle when working through issues. God is not even interested in your prayers if you are harsh. 1 Peter 3:7

131. When they are little, let your kids win games. If they don't win they will not like playing with you.

132. If you are a "black and white" person, you could be making someone feel discounted about 50% of the time. That's a lot.

133. Pray with your children before bed, but after talking about a difficult thing for them, take their hands in yours and pray. Aloud.

134. Know that your wife is your closest neighbor. Love her well. God says so.

135. Instead of engaging in conflict or talking about every little problem, ask God what you should address. Listen. Obey.

136. Don't be greedy. It brings trouble to your family. Proverbs 15:27

137. Know you are being foolish if you don't constantly work on growing and becoming more like Christ as a man. Proverbs 15:32

138. Know people learn more from encouragement than from complaining and criticizing.

139. God knows your motives. Ask Him to help you change them.

140. Don't start stupid arguments. Major in the majors and let the little things go. Give up having to be right. Proverbs 17:14

141. Stop disagreeing with stuff she says. It damages your relationship. Let her be wrong. Think, "so what?"

142.   Encourage her to go see her sister or friend, or whoever else is important to her every so often.
143.   Be responsible with money. Don't live in debt. Financial stability matters and is a sign of manhood.
144.   Teach the kids to work by making it fun and do it with them. Don't delegate, yell or expect perfection. Praise what they do well.
145.   Ask her to find you a good book on being a dad. Read it. Do what it says.
146.   Make this a motto: Say what you mean, mean what you say, keep your commitments.
147.   Are you still complaining? STOP. It is contagious. Look for what is good to avoid bad things. Proverbs 12:27
148.   Understand that wealth will not bring you happiness. Ask God to help you find balance between providing and family time.
149.   Don't argue in front of others. Know you might need to officially table discussion until you can talk through the issue.
150.   Stop taking things so personally. Focus on what is TRUE in any situation.
151.   Think before you speak – you wound your kids and wife when you don't. Proverbs 13:18
152.   Don't make angry and inconsiderate men your trusted, close friends or you may become like them. Proverbs 22:24
153.   Don't envy what others have. Pursue God instead and you and your family will be happy. Proverbs 23:17
154.   Tell the truth, gently, but don't lie. Proverbs 24:26

155.   Choose to admire men more mature in their faith than you, and make them your friends. Do not be intimidated by good men, but strive to be like them.

156.   Stop trying to make your wife or kids perfect. Be thankful and praise their strengths or you will demotivate them.

157.   Take care of your body. It's the temple of the Holy Spirit, and eating and drinking too much is the sin of gluttony. Proverbs 23:20

158.   Don't make a big deal out of your wife's or your kids' mistakes. Proverbs 17:9

159.   Laziness is a sin. Fix that thing she's been waiting on you to fix.

160.   Keep yourself clean and smelling fresh. This includes your breath. Always.

161.   Make time on a regular basis to be with just her. Plan something right now if it has been over a week since you have had a date.

162.   Don't put time with your friends over time with her. But make sure you are spending time with wise men to learn from them.

163.   Hold your tongue. Proverbs 13:3 says, "He who guards his lips guards his life, but he who speaks rashly will come to ruin."

164.   Hold her hand and smile at her in public. Do it when it is just the two of you, also. Make it a habit.

165.   When walking down the street, walk on the outside. Help her be safe and walk next to her so she feels like she's with you.

166. Make small affectionate effort daily. Touch her, smile at her, tell her she's pretty and that you can't live without her.
167. Model mature behavior by being the one to put your pride aside first. Be the first to admit fault, the first to apologize.
168. Your wife will need affection your whole marriage. Give her continual affection and romance. Daily. Occasionally pursue sex.
169. Know that if you only reward perfection instead of effort, your wife and kids will stop trying to please you.
170. If you are only satisfied with excellence instead of progress, people will stop trying. Praise Progress.
171. Tell the truth, but gently. And just because you have an opinion doesn't mean you need to share it. Avoid criticizing.
172. Know that those selfish feelings of, "I'm tired of being the one to change," are from the little boy in you – ask God to help you man up.
173. If she hurts you, pray, asking God if He wants you to overlook the hurt, or gently confront her sin against you. Forgive regardless.
174. Kiss her in public, if she is okay with that. Tell her, "I fall in love with you over and over again every day."
175. Pick up at home and have the kids do so also. Don't yell at them but have fun, or she worries about your being harsh.
176. Ask God to make you generous. Ask your wife to do something for someone you or she knows that is in need.

177.   Gently pull her hair back from the back of her neck and kiss it. Say, "You... are just beautiful."
178.   Ask your wife to teach you how to do your little girl's hair.
179.   Don't know what to do? GET ADVICE from wise men and your wife. Ask God what to do.
180.   Don't put off until tomorrow what you can do today. She admires proactive behavior.
181.   Serve your wife and your kids, starting with the youngest before serving yourself.
182.   Don't break the law. Do you lie to telemarketers? Speed? Kids catch more than they are taught.
183.   If you don't feel confident, act like you are anyway. Shake hands firmly. Make eye contact. Be a man. SMILE.
184.   Stop telling your wife and kids their imperfections. They know. They need encouragement, consequences, and love.
185.   Pray for your family daily. They need your intercession.
186.   Ask your wife and kids if they feel like nothing they do is good enough for you. CHANGE before it is too late.
187.   Get counseling for your own insecurities and feelings of failure – understand the way you perceive yourself impacts others.
188.   Celebrate with your kids and your wife when someone does something awesome.
189.   NEVER call her or your kids names. That is immature behavior. Avoid swear words as well. Model godly communication.

190. Text her, "I love you, and I know God chose you for me."
191. Offer to change the baby's diaper regularly – even say, "I got this," without asking. Make this a habit.
192. Cut yourself some slack today – extend grace to yourself. You are doing the best you can at this place in your walk with God.
193. Text her, "Just thinking about U. Makes me miss U."
194. Know that Christian fellowship isn't optional – it's biblical. Go to church. Get involved weekly with men.
195. Show her the photos you keep on your computer or phone of your family.
196. Make sure you have a family pic as your home screen. Send her a screen shot if you can.
197. If you are not constantly learning, growing, and changing, you have too much pride. Know it puts distance in your marriage.
198. Call her name from across the room, then say, "I just wanted to see your pretty face." Smile at her.
199. If you are tired, get rest. Burning yourself out puts a burden on your wife and kids.
200. Ask God to make you more gentle and kind toward the people you live and work with.
201. STOP fighting God. When trouble comes, don't resist it. Ask God what He's trying to teach you. Learn. Change.
202. When she's making dinner, come in the kitchen and offer to help. If you make dinner, stick around for clean-up.

203.   Text her, "I am so thankful I married you."
204.   Bring her a little gift. Do so once a month or so, especially if her love language is receiving gifts.
205.   Leave her a little note in her underwear drawer, something classy, like, "You are the one I want to spend forever with."
206.   Put "YOU are the most beautiful woman on the internet," on her Facebook wall.
207.   Hug her every day – and don't do it to get sex. If you only touch her when you want it, she'll feel used by you.
208.   How many things are "big deals" to you? Probably too many. Know this makes your wife think you are a hard man.
209.   Know that if you keep re-doing things that your wife or kids do, they will feel like failures and stop trying to please you.
210.   Avoid pornography. If you are addicted, get help. Teach your sons to do likewise.
211.   Put Covenant Eyes, Net Nanny, American Family Online, and/or BeSafe on your computer to avoid pornography, then have her control the password.
212.   Be proactive around the house. Don't wait for her to ask you five times for something, as it makes her feel like your mom.
213.   Be proactive about creating a budget together. Stretch goal – do Dave Ramsey's Financial Peace together and follow it.
214.   Send her a text that reads, "Can't wait 2 C U 2nite. Miss U, gorgeous."

215.   Take her shopping for a new outfit, or watch the kids while she goes to the store with a gift card from you.

216.   If you actually think you are better than anyone else, you are NOT thinking or acting like Jesus. Your wife knows this.

217.   Be interested in your kids and the day they had. Ask, "What did you do today? What was fun? What was hard?"

218.   If she is frugal, say, "Thanks for being careful about how you spend. You should treat yourself now and then, K?"

219.   Ask her to go for a walk with you. Hold her hand.

220.   If she is overweight, invite her to go on walks with you. Say, "It's a nice night, how about a romantic stroll?"

221.   If she ever walks out during an argument, go after her. Say, "I can't live without you, I'm sorry things escalated."

222.   Make dinner or give her the night off by bringing home take out.

223.   Stroke or brush her hair if she likes it.

224.   Text her, "Just a reminder that you are very much loved by me."

225.   Tell her, "I'm so privileged to have you in my life. I want to be the best man I can be for you and the kids."

226.   Treat your wife like you want a man to treat your daughter, and your sons to treat the mother of your grandkids.

227. Don't gossip about people you are upset with – talk TO them, working out the issues. Teach your kids this. It's admirable.

228. Notice when she has her arms full and say, "Hey, let me help you!" Then help.

229. If she complains about being exhausted, ask her, "I'm so sorry – what can I do to help?"

230. Don't trust and become close to men who are only interested in having a good time – their bad habits will rub off on you.

231. Trim your nails – and with clippers, not your teeth, and not in front of her.

232. If you have pets, help take care of them. Invite your wife to walk the dog with you. It's romantic.

233. If you get angry and lash out at children and pets for accidents, know that says more about you than it does about them.

234. Be nice to her mother. Don't complain about her mom, her sisters, or her friends to her.

235. If you have young kids, you should get up with them on the weekend so your wife can rest.

236. If you and your wife both work AND you have kids, you need to share in the night-time kid care.

237. Ask your wife if she'd like to work part-time or stay home with kids – then figure out with her how to live frugally and do it.

238. When she is sick, if you can, arrange your work around taking care of her and the kids, driving them places.

239. Never go through a door first, or leave her behind when you are out. Remember she is with you. Hold her hand.

240.   Help her with her coat.
241.   Text her, "How's your day going? Mine's full of thoughts about you."
242.   If she is having a crisis with a friend, listen to her woes. Nod your head. Tell her, "That has to be hard for you. So sorry."
243.   Add "I am sorry I hurt you," "I was wrong," "I'll not do this again," and "How can I make it up to you?" to your repertoire.
244.   When you are wrong, apologize quickly, admit you were wrong. Ask her to forgive you.
245.   Make eye contact with her when she is speaking.
246.   Do you love debate? Know it might be sin and harms your relationships. Proverbs 17:19
247.   Build your marriage and family with LOVE and not anger which creates fear. Be gentle and kind. Your wife respects that.
248.   Know that if you are controlling with your wife and kids, they will eventually want nothing to do with you.
249.   If you have daughters and sons, teach your boys how precious women are by coaching them with their sisters.
250.   Do not perform male body grooming where she can see, hear, or smell you.
251.   If she seems upset or angry, say, "You seem (upset/sad/angry), do you want to talk about it?"
252.   Teach your daughters and sons how a man treats a woman by treating your wife and daughters well in front of your boys.

253. Stay off your phone when you are with your family. Make eye contact and be a good listener instead.
254. When she says you hurt her feelings, say, "I'm sorry, help me understand," instead of arguing with her.
255. Hold your wife when she cries. Tell her you are sorry she is hurting. Even if it is not about you.
256. Encourage your wife and children daily by looking for whatever is good and telling them about it. 1 Thessalonians 5:11
257. When something happens to you (good or bad) TELL HER ABOUT IT. Don't keep things from her, or let her be surprised here.
258. Take a Sunday school class at your church with her.
259. Have an accountability group of men where you study ways to be better men. Don't stop doing this. Ever.
260. Hold her hand during worship or prayer time while at church together.
261. Go to church with her. Take your kids. Make it a thing you do every single Sunday no matter what.
262. Snuggle with your kids. They'll need your strong arms around them as long as they live. Don't stop hugging them.
263. Don't swear. Don't criticize. Don't complain. Use your words to build others up. Ephesians 4:29 style.
264. Put "YOU ROCK as a mom. I am the luckiest man on the planet," on her Facebook wall.

265. Decide now that you are going to be a stable, mature man. You won't be flighty, you'll man up to tough things. So will your sons.
266. Tell her, "You are precious to me. A gift. I was just thinking about how much better my life is because you are in it."
267. Ask her how her day went and really listen. Make this a habit.
268. Wink at her across the room.
269. Help her get the kids up and ready for church or school. If both of you work, do this often.
270. Help her schedule some time out with her friends or alone to recharge her batteries this week.
271. Hug your daughters, no matter what age they are. They need affection and appropriate male touch.
272. Be quiet when getting ready for work so she can get sleep (on average, women need more sleep than men).
273. Don't make large decisions without her input. Ask her what she would like to have more say in. Listen.
274. Periodically clean up the bathroom or kitchen when she is not around.
275. Ask her if you can watch the kids (or do a chore) so she can get a nap.
276. Give her a kiss after holding her car door open for her.
277. Leave her a note if you leave before she does that says, "I just want you to know I appreciate all you do."

278.   Buy a small chalkboard and leave an encouraging note or a verse for your family on it once in a while.

279.   Know that if you want honor, you have to die to your pride and become humble. Proverbs 15:33

280.   Smile. At her. At your kids. A lot.

281.   Look for what is happening around you that is going right or is good – and talk about that instead of complaining.

282.   Do not criticize her or something she did or something she's responsible for in front of the kids. Ever.

283.   Gently but firmly stand up for her with your kids.

284.   Ask her to pray for specific things you are going through, even daily.

285.   Ask her what you can pray for her about today. Then pray.

286.   Ask your wife if she wants your advice or help before you give it. She often just wants empathy instead.

287.   Work for God and not to impress others, even if your wife isn't impressed. Just do your best for God.

288.   Know you don't have to solve her problems. Listening and showing her empathy matters more to her sometimes.

289.   If you think arguing is fun, know you are inviting pain and sin into your relationships. Proverbs 19:17

290.   Text her, "Will you go out with me? ▨" Then set up something you know she loves to do.

291. Make a list of 30 things in the next minute that you did together when dating, then take time today to schedule them with her.
292. If you have an opinion about everything and share it, you are known as boorish. STOP. Be a good listener instead.
293. Lay down your need to be right. Pick your battles wisely, and only disagree about things that matter.
294. Pick her up off her feet and swing her around. Say, "Gosh, you are pretty."
295. Dance with her when there is no music. Start by hugging her while she's standing, then start swaying, then dance, even if you are klutzy.
296. Schedule an appointment with your doctor to take care of yourself.
297. Start exercising if you don't already.
298. Ask her if she thinks you are a responsible man. Act on her input. Don't argue with her, regardless of what she says.
299. Listen more than you speak in conversation, even with your kids. If you are the one doing all the talking...that's pride.
300. Get control of your anger, if you struggle with it. You push her and the kids away from you when you are harsh.
301. Ask her and your kids (if you drink) if you drink too much. Don't argue with their answer. If you do not drink, don't start.
302. Bring her coffee or tea (whatever she drinks) if she's been up all night with the baby and has to stay up.

303.   Ask her to recommend a great book on being a dad. Read it with your men's group. Apply what you learn.

304.   If she is disrespectful, take her hand and say, "I know you are hurting here, let's talk through this together." Be patient.

305.   Offer to take the baby so she can sleep. If both of you work, share night-time kid-care responsibilities.

306.   Thank her on her Facebook wall for doing something with the kids recently.

307.   Call her during the day and say, "I just called to say I love you!"

308.   Ask her to coach you on baby care activities. Tell her you want to be good at it.

309.   Say, "You are a great wife, and I don't know what I'd do without you."

310.   Ask her, "Is there anything I can do around the house this weekend? A project you need done?" Then do it.

311.   Text her, "I was just remembering my favorite vacation with you. We should do that again."

312.   Nuzzle her neck while hugging her.

313.   Carry the laundry baskets up the stairs or to the bedrooms for her. Better yet, put them away and put the baskets back.

314.   If you pay the bills, make sure you do so on time, so that she doesn't get phone calls about it.

315.   Always thank her for making dinner, finding something to compliment her about. If you criticize, she'll stop trying.

316. Brush your teeth and keep your breath fresh. Use deodorant.
317. Your wife wants to hear what you are struggling with. Tell her and ask her to pray for you. Ask her for her thoughts, too.
318. Brush her lips with your finger, then trace her jawline. Say, "You are so pretty. I love looking at your face."
319. Run out and get milk when you run low without her asking you to.
320. Stare at her until she notices. Say, "I can't stop looking at you." Smile.
321. Offer to take the kids where they need to go in the evening so she can get a break.
322. Say to your kids, "I was just thinking about how lucky I am to have married your mother! Don't you think she's great?"
323. Know the best days of your life occur when you have grandkids. They haven't happened yet.
324. No matter what, give 10%, save 10%, and try to live off your income alone, so that the choice to have more kids is not affected.
325. Pray before dinner. Share what God is doing in your life with your kids. Ask them how they are experiencing Him.
326. Ask God to help you know Him more, to help obey Him.
327. Nibble on her ear, then kiss her. Say, "I love you more and more each day."
328. Ask her what her idea of the perfect vacation is, then start saving to make it happen.

329. Ask God to reveal to you if you do things of immature or questionable character. Then ask Him to help you be a man of integrity.
330. Be humble. If you talk about yourself, play yourself down, not up. Brag about your wife and kids to your wife and kids.
331. If you don't like something or are angry, be careful how or IF you speak about it. Don't discourage those around you.
332. NEVER call your kids or your wife names unless they are positive and affirming. Like "beautiful" or "tough guy," or "princess."
333. Ditch the sarcasm. It usually backfires as humor and makes you appear immature.
334. If you are doing most of the talking, people are not impressed. Be interested in others instead and you'll be appreciated.
335. Fear and respect God. It's the beginning of wisdom.
336. Be careful about what you share with others.
337. Be generous with your time, your money, and your affection with the people who matter the most to you. First.
338. Pay attention to what your wife and kids are doing right today. TELL THEM those things instead of criticizing or complaining.
339. Be a man with a long fuse. It will improve your reputation and relationships with literally everyone.
340. Insist that she take time to read, spend time with her friends, or whatever else fills her up.
341. Remember that no matter what you DO, you do it for God, not for her reactions or lack thereof.

342. Text her, "What do I do that makes you feel loved the most?" Then do that more often.

343. Have enough friends that if you died tomorrow, your wife will have an abundance of men to ask to carry your casket.

344. Daily compliment each one of your kids' – focus on character traits. You are building or tearing down with your words.

345. Tidy up the kitchen after dinner so your wife doesn't have to.

346. Know that the anger you feel toward someone else's failings is often because you have the same issue. Give grace.

347. Schedule a man's getaway with your guy friends and their sons. Don't feel guilty about going. You need to. Stay pure while gone.

348. Understand that appreciation has the power to transform a person. Give appreciation daily to your people.

349. Buy her a small jewelry item now and again if she likes it. Say, "I saw this and thought it would be pretty on you."

350. If her shoes are scuffed, polish them for her without saying anything about it.

351. Do things for her without expecting gratitude or reward. You are modeling Christ-like behavior.

352. When she complains, empathize. Ask her if there is anything you can do to help.

353. When at dinner in a restaurant, stare at her. Say, "You are the most stunning woman here tonight."

354. If her neck hurts, rub it. If her feet hurt, rub them.

355. Text her, "I'm so glad you are our kids' mom. You really know them."

356. Dip her backwards when you kiss her today. Smile wildly at her.

357. Fix that thing she's been wanting you to fix.

358. Say, "I'm happy for you!" and "That has to be hard for you," to your family members daily as appropriate.

359. If your wife makes you dinner, say "thank you!" even if you didn't like all of it. Be critical and she'll lose her enthusiasm.

360. Check your face. Are you smiling? The more you smile at your wife and in your home, the happier SHE will be with life.

361. Stop bickering over small stuff. Proverbs 20:3 says, "It is to a man's honor to avoid strife, but every fool is quick to quarrel."

362. Don't brag about yourself. Let others' praise you and you'll receive honor. Proverbs 27:2

363. If you think you are wise, you are actually arrogant. Proverbs 26:12

364. Stand up for those who cannot stand up for themselves. Your kids and your wife will admire you.

365. Good godly men don't take advantage of others at work or home. Proverbs 28:18

Ephesians 5:33 tells us, "*However, let each one of you love his wife as himself, and let the wife see that she respects her husband."* 1 Peter 3:7 says, *"Likewise, husbands, live with your wives in an understanding way, showing honor to the woman as the weaker vessel, since they are heirs with you of the grace of life, so that your prayers may not be hindered."*

What communicates *"I love you" to your wife? Don't know? ASK her. Want to score some quick "points?" Try, "Honey, I'm so sorry I've hurt you over the years. I have struggled with how to love you well. Please forgive me. I want to try to do better. I love you – will you give me another chance?"* **Then change. Because apology with change is a reflection of high integrity.** Apology without change is, well, not. And keep your eyes on YOUR behavior, and not hers, avoiding the sin of judgment. She has her own walk with God. Chances are she's working on it, too. Dare you to then do these things. It will make a huge difference in your relationship. We also want you to feel welcome on my blog – we appreciate the men who chime in now and again with insightful comments. I'm also available to speak to groups. You can contact us through our website at GreaterImpact.org.

Respectfully,

~Nina

Want Nina to Speak at Your Event?

Nina has seen God's hand at work in the courses and books He's inspired her to write. Over 95 percent of her participants report improving their relationship with God and becoming more confident. She firmly believes that to be fully productive and have peace, one must live life for the audience of One, being fully engaged in all the roles He has placed us in. She has found her calling in leaving secular business to write and deliver courses for Christians at a fraction of the cost of what the same high caliber of training goes for in the marketplace.

Nina has over 20 years in the communications and training industry including 15 years with the largest and most successful training company in the world. She has coached numerous executives and pastors around the country and currently provides leadership for Greater Impact Ministries, Inc. as Executive Director.

Nina's expertise in the classroom as a facilitator, trainer, and coach display her God given talents. She and her husband, Jim, met in 1985 and married in 1991 after Nina finished her Masters degree at West Virginia University. She and Jim are privileged to be raising their 3 children, Adam, Bram and Elizabeth, together in Loveland, Ohio. Nina can be booked for speaking engagements through the ministry website at http://www.GreaterImpact.org.

There is more...

Have you ever wondered, "Isn't there more?"

Like something is missing?

There is.

We can help you find it. That's what we're all about. You're not meant to do this on your own. God created us to rely on Him, but we don't. We fight it. We think we can do it by ourselves and that maybe God will be proud of us when we figure it out.

Here's the truth: He wants to do it with us. Through us. He has a plan for each of us.

Join us and receive training, teaching, and knowledge that will change how you live your life. We listen and offer feedback, and celebrate with you as God does truly big stuff. **With Him, you can make a greater impact**. In your marriage. With your children. At your workplace.

Join us and discover your more.

- Retreats
- Workshops
- Courses

GreaterImpact™

Redefining training to redefine lives.

554 Belle Meade Farm Drive * Loveland, Ohio 45140 * 513.310.6019 * www.greaterimpact.org